CORAL REEFS IN DANGER

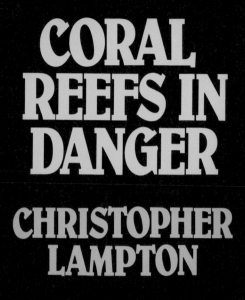

CORAL REEFS IN DANGER

CHRISTOPHER LAMPTON

The Millbrook Press
Brookfield, Connecticut

Cover photo courtesy of Superstock

Photos courtesy of Superstock: pp. 2–3, 10, 21, 22, 29, 54;
Photo Researchers: pp. 8 (James T. Spencer), 18 and 42
(Andrew J. Martinez), 33 (Gregory Dimijian), 38 (Fred
McConnaughey), 41 (Nancy Sefton), 48 (top, Garry D.
McMichael; bottom, Science Source/Giss); Peter Arnold:
pp. 12, 17, 34 (Jeffrey L. Rotman), 19 (Norbert Wu), 26
30 (Fred Bavendam); U.S. Department of Energy: p. 53.

Library of Congress Cataloging-in-Publication Data

Lampton, Christopher.
Coral reefs in danger / by Christopher Lampton.
p. cm.
Includes bibliographical references and index.
Summary: Describes the formation of a coral reef, its ecosystem, and the current problem of dying reefs—possibly
caused by global warming.
ISBN 1-56294-091-0 (lib. bdg.)
1. Coral reef ecology. 2. Coral reef biology. [1. Coral
reefs and islands. 2. Coral reef ecology.] I. Title.
QH541.5.C7L36 1992
574.5'26367—dc20   91-41441 CIP AC

CONTENTS

CORAL REEFS IN DANGER

INTRODUCTION

It's a beautiful morning in the Caribbean.
You sit on the deck of a boat as it cruises
among the Bahama Islands and begin to pull
on your scuba gear in preparation for a dive.
All around you stretches the beautifully clear
water for which the tropics are famous. You
think about the last dive that you made here,
a year earlier, and recall the beautiful coral
reef that is even now below the boat. You
remember the marvelous variety of plants
and fish. In particular, you remember the
amazing formations of the coral itself, in a
wild variety of colors.

Colors. That's what you mostly remember—startlingly bright reds, oranges, pur-
ples, yellows, and browns.

You slip a pair of flippers onto your feet
and lower yourself over the side of the boat,
into the warm waters. Gently, you descend

A coral reef is home to a wide variety of brilliantly colored plants and fish.

below the surface, breathing air from the tank strapped to your back. You begin to make your way down toward the coral reef.

But something is wrong. Before you've descended more than a few feet, you pass through a strange cloud of dark particles. Where did these come from, you wonder. Last year the waters had seemed so clear!

You dive below the cloud of particles and look for the coral reef. It is still there, but something is wrong with it. The color is gone. The reef, with its strange, twisted shape, is still there—but it is white. Pure white. It is like a blanket of snow on the bottom of the ocean, stretching as far as the eye can see.

What happened to the reef, you wonder. Everything seems so strange, so different. A sense of alarm begins to come over you and you begin swimming up to the surface. You climb onto the boat and tell the others what you have seen. At first they don't believe you, but when they lean over the side of the boat and look down into the water, they see it, too. The reef has become white. Something is very wrong here.

The reef has been . . . bleached!

The above scene is fiction, but the bleaching of the reefs is in fact happening right now. Something is killing the coral reefs of the world—and nobody is quite sure what it is.

But scientists have theories. And if these theories are correct, the strange fate that is befalling coral reefs around the world may be a sign of stranger and more terrible things to come.

The reefs may be telling us that the climate of the planet Earth is changing. If this is so, then it will affect more than just coral reefs. It will affect the entire world and the people who live in it.

What is killing the coral reefs of the world? In this book, we'll try to answer that question. And we'll ask a couple of questions of our own: Is it too late to save the coral reefs? And, what does the dying of the reefs signify for the rest of the world?

A school of anthias around a coral reef in the Red Sea.

CHAPTER ONE

THE REEF BUILDERS

What is a reef? To a sailor, it is a submerged hazard, an underwater obstacle that can rip the bottom right out of a ship. It lies too far below the waves to be easily seen, yet it is not submerged deeply enough for a ship to pass safely over it. To a sailor, a coral reef is a disaster waiting to happen.

To a diver, however, a reef can be a place of great beauty. Here schools of exotic fish swim among strange and beautiful plants, all clustered around unusual formations that look like a kind of stone. It is a place to which divers come again and again to experience its breathtaking loveliness.

And to a scientist, a reef is a kind of puzzle, a lesson in biology and ecology that holds many secrets, only some of which are fully understood. This book is about such a secret, a secret held by certain reefs that may, when understood, provide an answer to one of the most important questions of our time: Are we in the process of destroying our own planet?

The most interesting reefs are those made of a substance called *coral*. Coral reefs are found only in the tropical regions between the equator and the tropic of Cancer to the north, and the tropic of Capricorn to the south. Coral reefs take many forms. One type of reef lies just off the shore of a continent or island, while another type is found several miles from the nearest shore. Yet another type forms mysterious rings in the middle of the ocean, far from any land. In some cases, whole islands are made of coral.

But what *is* coral? Is it animal, vegetable, or mineral? That's a tougher question than you might think. In fact, you might at first assume that coral must be mineral, since it's difficult to imagine an entire island made out of something that is alive. But you would be wrong. Coral is very much alive.

You might be tempted to guess instead that coral is a vegetable, a kind of hard-shelled plant that lives at the bottom of the water. If you saw a living coral, or a picture of one, you would be even more tempted to guess that it's some sort of plant. Certain types of coral, especially the so-called *soft corals*, look like spectacular species of seaweed, waving like fronds in the water. But you would be wrong again.

In fact, coral is an animal. That may be hard to believe, since a typical coral animal spends most of its life anchored to the bottom of the ocean or to other corals that are in turn anchored to the ocean bottom. But an animal it is. After settling down at an early age, it never budges from the spot where it has attached itself. And yet it is capable of building structures that are larger than those created by any other creatures on Earth, structures that can be seen from far out in space. Visitors from another planet, flying toward Earth in their spaceships, would be able to see coral reefs long before they could see such man-made structures as the skyscrapers of New York City or the Egyptian pyramids. But amazingly, these reefs were built by tiny creatures that spend their entire lives under the sea.

A coral reef is actually a coral *colony*, a family of coral animals living together in an ever-growing mass. In its newborn (or *larval*) stage, the coral animal is called a *planula*. The planula is shaped a little like a pear and can swim through water by wiggling tiny hairs that line the sides of its body. The planula may swim for hours or days or even weeks after it is born. But eventually it finds a hard surface to which it attaches itself. It will never move from that spot again in its life.

Once attached, it turns into a *polyp*, which is the adult form of the coral animal. It begins to develop a tiny slit of a mouth, around which tentacles start to grow. It also grows a skeleton—*outside* its body. The form that it takes as an adult basically depends on the type of coral it is.

Corals are divided loosely into two types: *hard* (or *stony*) *corals* and *soft corals*. There are two major areas of difference between these types of corals. As the names imply, the hard corals have a hard skeleton surrounding their bodies while the soft corals have a soft skeleton.

An adult hard coral consists of a polyp inside a hard, cup-shaped skeleton. At the top of the cup is the polyp's mouth, surrounded by tentacles. For much of the day, these tentacles are folded up tightly against the polyp's body. But at night, they shoot out into the water, looking for food.

What do coral polyps eat? Mostly, they eat the tiny plants and animals known as *plankton*, which float through the night waters in large numbers. The tentacles trap the plankton, then draw it into the polyp's mouth. Occasionally, the coral polyp will trap small fish that pass a little too close to its mouth. Poisonous stingers in the tentacles paralyze these creatures long enough for the polyp to swallow and begin to digest them.

Soft corals are similar to hard corals, but they tend to live deeper beneath the water, where plankton comes out in the daytime rather than at night. Hence, the soft corals feed during the day while the hard corals feed at night.

Eventually, the adult polyp reproduces by budding off a new polyp. These young polyp buds grow from the sides of the old polyps, forming hard skeletons of their own as they reach adulthood. They never detach themselves from the "parent" polyp. (Polyps can also reproduce sexually, producing the planula that start the colonies, but the colonies grow only by budding.)

In this way, the coral colony slowly grows, polyp by polyp, bud by bud. Some types of corals form their colonies in a gradually expanding, symmetrical mass. One of the most striking of these colonies is formed by the so-called *brain corals*, which resemble the convolutions of a human brain. Other corals branch like the antlers of a moose or deer—hence the name *staghorn coral*.

There are many other varieties of corals. *Lettuce-leaf coral*, for instance, has a leafy appearance resembling the vegetable it is named for. *Fire coral* gets its name from special cells on the skin of the polyps that poison the flesh of any animal (including humans) that comes in contact with it. It causes an intense stinging sensation. The *gorgonian corals* form twisted branches that look like the snake-haired gorgons of Greek mythology.

The soft corals, as the name implies, are more flexible than the hard corals. A diver swimming among soft corals might be forgiven for believing that he or she had wandered into an underwater garden filled with a variety of exotic plants! *Sea fans* and *tree corals*, for instance, look like brightly colored underwater trees without leaves.

This coral polyp has its tentacles open for feeding.

Red gorgonian corals wave gracefully in the waters of the South Pacific.

Staghorn coral branches look like the antlers of a moose or deer.

As previously mentioned, colonies of coral grow at a moderate rate. It may take a brain coral colony 20 years to double its size. Staghorn coral adds only a few feet to its length each year. But given enough time, a coral reef can grow very large.

There are three basic kinds of coral reefs: *fringing reefs*, *barrier reefs*, and *atolls*. A fringing reef is a reef that borders a landmass, such as an island or a continent. It usually lies between about 150 to 1,500 feet (about 45 to 450 meters) from the shore. The stretch of water between the fringing reef and the shore is called a *lagoon*. Because the reef robs waves of their energy as they rush toward shore, lagoon water is usually much more calm than the open sea.

The fringing reef itself is divided up into several *zones*. The part of the reef facing into the lagoon is called the *back reef*. It is only slightly higher than the floor of the lagoon itself. The back reef leads upward to the *reef flat*, a long flat area, which in turn leads up to the highest point of the reef called the *reef crest*. The edge of the reef facing away from the lagoon is called the *reef front*, or *reef edge*. Below this edge is the *upper reef slope*, where most of the life on the reef is found. And below the upper reef slope is the *lower reef slope*, which continues downward to the seabed.

Barrier reefs are like fringing reefs, except that they are found a lot farther out to sea, from about ½ to 3 miles (almost 1 to 5 kilometers) from shore. The zones of a barrier reef are similar to those of a fringing reef. However, barrier reefs are usually found in deeper water, and are wider and higher than fringing reefs.

Finally, an atoll is a reef or system of reefs found far from any land. Usually, it forms a circle, rather like a fringing reef surrounding an island that isn't there. Instead, there is a *central lagoon* in the middle of the system.

The largest collection of fringing reefs in the world is found along the edges of the Red Sea, the 1,300-mile-long (almost 2,100-

Fringing reefs, like this one off Fiji, usually border an island or a continent.

The Great Barrier Reef north of Australia, is the world's largest coral reef.

kilometer) body of water that separates Africa from Asia. The most famous reef is the Great Barrier Reef just north of Australia, the largest structure ever built by living creatures. Atolls are common in the South Pacific.

Scientists have little trouble explaining how a fringing reef develops. The coral animals attach themselves to the ocean bottom just off shore, then form colonies that eventually become the reef. The action of waves and plant life also help to shape the reef.

Barrier reefs and atolls are something of a mystery. They tend to be found in deeper water than the fringing reefs. But coral does not like to grow at depths greater than about 150 feet (45 meters) below the water. How, then, do these deep-water reefs develop?

The first major theory of the development of barrier reefs and atolls was put forward in 1842 by the famous English naturalist Charles Darwin. His answer to the question of how reefs could form in deep water was simple. He proposed that, once upon a time, the water wasn't as deep.

Perhaps, Darwin suggested, the water level has risen over the years, so that reefs that are now in deep water were once in shallow water. The lower sea levels would have left much of what is now seafloor exposed as dry land. Thus, what are now barrier reefs and atolls would have once been fringing reefs.

As the water level gradually rose, the reefs would have become submerged deeper below the waves. At the same time, the shores that they fringed would have disappeared underwater. But the water level rose so slowly that the coral colonies were able to grow upward, through budding. Each reef kept growing so that it remained close to the surface. The lowest portions of these reefs consist only of the skeletons of dead polyps, but these support the living polyps that are still building the reefs today.

Although it was proposed 150 years ago, Darwin's theory is regarded as largely correct by modern scientists. A few new twists have been added, but Darwin's view has been proved over the years by studies of the underlying structures of reefs.

A reef is a great deal more than just a colony of coral organisms. It is a fascinating environment in which many different kinds of life-forms, both plant and animal, can live. And because the reefs are so full of living things, it is important that something be done about whatever mysterious force is endangering them.

CHAPTER TWO

THE WEB OF LIFE

All living things on Earth are connected. The air that animals breathe out becomes the air that plants breathe in. The fruits that grow on plants become the foods that are eaten by animals. And the animals in turn spread the seeds that are hidden in the fruit. In a sense, all living organisms are dependent on all other living organisms in a very complex way.

The study of the ways in which organisms live together is called *ecology*. An ecologist—a scientist who studies ecology—knows that the only way to understand fully life on Earth is not just to study individual life-forms, but to study *all* living things on Earth as they relate to one another.

Nowhere is this more true than in the environment of a coral reef. More different kinds of life are found on a coral reef than in any other environment on Earth, except for

Different species of damselfish swim among the coral formations of a reef off Australia.

the tropical rain forests of Africa and South America. Competition
among the reef organisms is fierce and constant, but cooperation is
necessary, too. Every plant or animal in the reef is adapted for eking
out a particular kind of living in the reef environment. And many of
these plants and animals depend on one another for their continued
existence.

Before we look at the ecology of the coral reef, however, let's
talk briefly about how a complex ecology like this can come about. It
is a story that begins literally billions of years ago, when the Earth
was still quite young.

The planet Earth has been around for more than 4.5 billion
years, and there has been life on this planet for most of that time.
The earliest living organisms, however, were not much like those
found on the planet today. In fact, they were little more than strings
of atoms (the tiny building blocks of all matter), floating in the
primeval seas.

These strings of atoms, however, had "learned" a clever trick,
purely by accident. They were able to make copies of themselves,
using the raw materials floating around in the water. Thus, their
number increased rapidly. However, these organisms occasionally
made errors in copying themselves, and sometimes these copies
were improvements on the originals. Because these improved copies
were more efficient at making copies of themselves, they soon came
to outnumber (and eventually replace) the originals.

This process is still going on today. Every living organism is a
distant descendant of the original strings of atoms. We now can
make copies of ourselves through a process called *reproduction*. Every time a new organism is born, be it a baby, a tree seedling, a
tadpole, or a bear cub, the parent has made a copy of itself. But
sometimes the new arrivals are improvements over their parents.
Eventually, these improvements will be passed on to many new

generations and the improved versions will outnumber the original. When organisms improve over time in this way, we say that they have *evolved*.

For instance, giraffes have adapted to their environment by evolving long necks, so that they can eat food that other animals can't reach. But a giraffe with an even longer neck can eat more food than other giraffes. So a giraffe with a longer neck would be an improvement over the standard version.

There are lots of ways that an organism can adapt to its environment, however. Each of these ways is called an *ecological niche*. An organism's ecological niche consists of the place, or *habitat*, in which it lives and the way it obtains food within that habitat. The habitat in which a giraffe lives, for instance, is the tropical grassland of Africa known as a savanna. The giraffe feeds on the tender shoots at the tops of trees that dot the savanna.

As organisms adapt to their environment, they must also adapt to the other organisms in that environment. Animals, for instance, eat other organisms in their environment. Some animals (called *carnivores*) eat other animals. Some animals (called *herbivores*) eat plants. Still other animals (called *omnivores*) eat both.

The single most important interrelationship between living organisms within any environment is the *food chain*, also sometimes known as the *food web*. All living organisms require energy in order to survive. It is energy that allows them to move and to perform the processes that keep them alive.

When we look at the plants and animals that live in and around a coral reef, we see many striking examples of the interrelationships between living creatures. One of the most fascinating is the relationship between the coral polyps and tiny organisms that live within their bodies, called *zooxanthellae*, from the Greek words meaning "little yellow creatures."

This aptly named harlequin shrimp is part of the web of life on a coral reef.

This unusual leather coral gets its green color from symbiotic algae.

Despite this name, the zooxanthellae are not creatures but ≈ **31** plants. They are a type of alga that lives in the stomachs of coral polyps. Thousands of zooxanthellae can make their home inside a single polyp.

Why would the zooxanthellae choose to live inside coral polyps? Why, for that matter, would the polyps allow them to do so? This is an example of the ecological phenomenon known as *symbiosis*, which can be explained by the popular saying, "I'll scratch your back if you scratch mine." Both the polyps and the zooxanthellae get something important out of the relationship.

The polyp provides the zooxanthellae with a safe home, away from the violence of the waves and the hungry jaws of herbivorous (plant-eating) fish. Enough light filters down through the water so that the zooxanthellae can capture the sun's energy and convert it into *carbohydrates* within the polyp's stomach through the process of *photosynthesis*. The zooxanthellae also acquire additional nutrition from the waste eliminated by the polyp.

The polyp, in turn, uses some of the carbohydrate energy created by the zooxanthellae as a dietary supplement. Although the polyp feeds nightly on passing plankton and the occasional fish, there just isn't enough of this food to keep an entire coral colony nourished. Hence, the "tiny yellow creatures" in the polyp's stomach provide it with essential nutrition. Without the zooxanthellae, the polyp would eventually starve.

And without the polyps, other organisms may starve as well. The *ecosystem* of the reef is the complete set of relationships between the organisms—plants, fish, and everything else—that live there. Perhaps the single most important set of relationships in the reef environment are those that make up the reef's food chain. The food chain in the reef begins primarily with the zooxanthellae that live inside the polyps. This means that the relationship between the polyps and their zooxanthellae is important not only to this pair of species, but to all the animals living in the reef. Without the zooxanthellae producing food from sunlight, many animals would starve, including the polyps themselves. Furthermore, the polyps create the reef itself, which serves as habitat for the many animals that live there. Without the polyps to build this habitat, there would be no place for these animals to live. Thus, if something were to happen to the polyps and their zooxanthellae, the entire reef ecosystem would fall apart.

Here are some other relationships in the world of the coral reef:

≈   *Anemones and clown fish.* The anemone is a close relative of the coral polyp and is commonly found near a coral reef. Like the polyp, its tentacles have poisonous stingers that can trap and kill small fish. However, the clown fish (so called for its bold colors and markings) lives among the tentacles of certain species of anemones. Because the tentacles keep larger fish away, the anemone keeps the clown fish safe from predators. But how does the clown fish protect itself from the deadly lash of the anemone? It covers itself with the same mucous that covers much of the anemone. The anemone is fooled into thinking that the clown fish is part of its own body! Scientists don't know if the anemone receives any benefits from its relationship to the clown fish.

≈   *Cleaning wrasses and cleaning gobies.* Small fish often eat smaller fish. Yet the tiny cleaning wrasses and cleaning gobies can swim right into the mouth of larger fish and eat the food from between their teeth! How do the wrasses and gobies get away with this? The large fish seem to consider this a public service. In effect, the wrasses and gobies are the dentists of the reef ecosystem! They clean parasites and dead tissue out of the mouths of the big fish, in return for

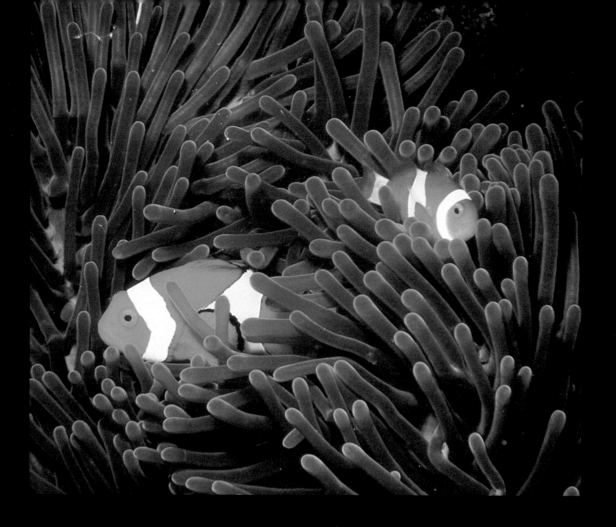

*The colorful clown fish
lives among the tentacles of
a certain type of anemone.*

Coral polyps are very sensitive to their environment.

which they get all the scraps of food they can eat. Large fish often line up at the "cleaning stations" established by these smaller fish.

These are just two examples of the reef ecosystem in action. It has evolved over a period of many millions of years, and the creatures that live within it have adapted almost perfectly to the environment.

But what if something were to come along and disturb this intricate ecosystem?

The living organisms that we see around us today have been adapting to their environments for, in some cases, many millions of years. What happens if the environments to which these organisms have adapted suddenly change? Then they may die out and be replaced by better-adapted life-forms. Or, if the change in the environment is slow enough, the organisms may evolve to fit it better. Fortunately, most changes within environments tend to be rather slow. Rapid changes are not unheard of, however. For instance, it is now believed that the dinosaurs (and many other organisms that lived on Earth 65 million years ago) died out after a large object struck the planet and altered the environment so seriously that few life-forms could adapt in time.

The coral reefs are a delicately balanced environment. The coral polyps, in particular, are very sensitive to their environment.

As we saw earlier, there is a greater variety of life-forms found in and around a coral reef than anywhere else on Earth, except the rain forests of Africa and South America. Tragically, the rain forests are being slowly destroyed to make room for farmland, and the life-forms in them are being destroyed as well. Huge numbers of species are becoming extinct as these forests disappear.

If some similar disaster were to strike the coral reefs, a large number of living species would vanish. And it would take only a small change to the reef environment to throw its delicate ecology off balance and bring about such a disaster.

And, in fact, there is evidence that such a disaster is occurring right now. There is reason to believe that coral reefs around the world will soon be dying in great numbers. Furthermore, this dying of the reefs may be caused by changes that people are making in the environment, changes that may eventually spell disaster for more than just coral reefs!

CHAPTER THREE

THE DYING OF THE REEFS

One of the first things that people notice when they visit the tropics is the color of the seawater. Sometimes it appears as a shimmering blue, other times as an opalescent green. Yet, when examined close up or scooped into a container, the water has no color at all.

What gives the tropical seas their colors? Often, it is the coral at the bottom, viewed through the perfectly transparent water above. One of the most striking things about coral is its color, which can be quite vivid and beautiful.

But every now and then a coral reef becomes *bleached*—that is, it loses its color the way that a bright red T-shirt can lose its color when washed in laundry bleach. This phenomenon was first noticed nearly a century ago, though at the time it was considered quite rare.

Bleached of its brilliant colors, a dying reef has a ghostly appearance.

What causes coral bleaching? As discussed in the last chapter, every coral polyp coexists in its skeleton with thousands of tiny organisms, called zooxanthellae, that live in the polyp's stomach. Among other things, these tiny plants provide the coral with the pigments that give them their color. If the polyps lose their zooxanthellae, the coral reverts to its natural color, usually white.

What would cause a polyp to lose its zooxanthellae? No one is quite sure, but scientists believe that polyps may expel their zooxanthellae in times of stress. What could cause coral polyps to become stressed? Changes in the environment, usually. Changes in water temperature or the amount of salt in the water or even the presence of pollution in the water can disturb the usually peaceful existence of the polyp.

If these stressful changes should somehow prevent the zooxanthellae inside the polyp from gathering energy from the sun, then the zooxanthellae will no longer be able to maintain a symbiotic relationship with the polyp. The polyp might then reject the zooxanthellae, because it will cost the polyp more energy to support the zooxanthellae than it will receive from it in return.

Should the stressful conditions go away within a few days or weeks, the polyp can then ingest new zooxanthellae and go about its business as usual. But if the stressful conditions last for a longer time—several months or years, perhaps—the polyp will probably die of malnutrition. It will not be able to obtain enough nourishment from plankton and passing small fish to survive long term. Furthermore, repeated bleachings will so weaken the polyp that even a short bleaching may eventually bring about its death. Thus an entire coral reef can—in theory, anyway—starve to death.

And if the coral polyps die the reef will stop growing. The ecosystem of the reef will fall apart. Organisms dependent on the polyps will die, and in turn this will spell the end for their dependent organisms. If all of this occurs gradually, the life-forms that live in the reef may adapt to changing conditions. But if it occurs rapidly, thousands of species may die in one fell swoop.

Has such a thing ever happened? Has an entire reef system ever died as the result of a bleaching—or is one likely to die in the near future? Most bleachings are quite temporary, but in the 1980s many coral bleachings began occurring around the world. The first major bleaching episode was in 1980, with another following three years later, in 1983. A third occurred in 1987 and yet another in 1990. Furthermore, each bleaching seemed to be worse, or at least longer lasting, than the previous. Although the reefs have survived all of the bleachings so far, this may not be the case in the future.

What is causing these bleachings? Scientists have considered many possible explanations. Here are some of the possibilities:

≈ *Disease.* Perhaps some organism has infected the reefs and is slowly killing them off. This explanation is considered unlikely. Bleachings have occurred simultaneously in the Caribbean Sea and in the Pacific Ocean, which are literally half a world apart. How could any pathogen (disease-causing organism) spread that quickly? Furthermore, pathogens tend to be very selective, striking only a few species. Yet, whatever is causing the bleaching of the reefs affects a wide variety of coral species as well as several types of anemones and sponges. Interestingly, these anemones and sponges are also hosts to zooxanthellae.

≈ *Damage by divers.* Coral reefs tend to be popular spots for deep-sea divers, both amateur and professional. Could unwanted attention from these ocean tourists be damaging the coral reefs, causing the bleachings? Once again, while this could cause local bleachings, it seems unlikely that divers would be responsible for a pattern of bleachings around the world at the same time.

≈   *Salinity*. A sudden rise in the salt content of the water could cause the polyps to expel their zooxanthellae. Polyps are extremely sensitive to the salt content of the water in which they live, but there is no evidence of a worldwide rise in the salt content of the oceans.

≈   *Ultraviolet light*. Exposure to ultraviolet light can cause zoo-xanthellae to lose the pigment that gives the coral its color. But it doesn't kill the zooxanthellae nor does it cause them to be expelled from the polyps. Since the evidence indicates that the polyps are actually losing their zooxanthellae, ultraviolet light doesn't seem a likely culprit.

≈   *Pollution*. An increase in water pollution, or of sediment in the water, could block the sunlight reaching the polyps and thus prevent the zooxanthellae from performing photosynthesis. This in turn could cause the polyps to eject the zooxanthellae. But there is no evidence that all the bleached reefs are in areas of unusual pollution or sedimentation.

Of course, just because these and other factors aren't causing the mass bleaching, that doesn't mean that they aren't damaging the reefs or even causing occasional local bleachings. There are many ways in which reefs can become damaged. Pollution and increased levels of silt have been responsible for the deaths of many reef organisms, especially the sensitive polyps and their zooxanthellae. During the recent war in the Persian Gulf, oil dumped into the waters there by the Iraqis has caused substantial damage to reefs in that part of the world. But these factors can probably be dismissed as the cause of the large-scale reef bleachings that are threatening reefs worldwide.

If all of these possibilities were ruled out, what would be left? Some scientists have been zeroing in on a single explanation for the bleaching of the reefs: increased water temperature. Coral polyps can thrive only within a limited range of water temperatures. This, in fact, is why reefs are found only in a narrow region around the equator, where water temperatures are in an acceptable range. Even a slight increase in temperature has been known to cause polyps to expel their zooxanthellae and become bleached. A year in which the global weather is unusually warm could be responsible for a sudden wave of worldwide coral bleaching. Although not all scientists agree with this theory, many believe that this is what is happening.

What if the bleaching of the reefs is caused by more than just a brief heat wave? What if the weather around the globe is actually changing permanently, or at least for an extended period of time? What if things get hotter and stay that way? What will happen to the reefs then?

We can only guess, of course, but the future doesn't look good for the coral reefs. If the change in weather occurs rapidly enough, so that the reef environment doesn't have a chance to adapt, it may mean that reefs around the world will die. And when they die, the thousands of species of plants and animals that live among the reefs may become extinct.

Is there any reason to believe that the world may be getting warmer? Unfortunately, there is. In fact, scientists have been predicting this possibility for many years. If they are correct, the dying of the reefs could be an early warning sign of a drastic change in our weather that may affect far more than just reefs.

As we will see in the next chapter, this may signal the beginning of a worldwide greenhouse effect.

CHAPTER FOUR

LIFE IN THE GREENHOUSE

The term *climate* refers to long-term weather. If the weather where you live tends to be warm and dry, then we say you live in a warm, dry climate. If the weather where you live tends to be cold and wet, we say you live in a cold, wet climate. That doesn't mean that the weather is warm and dry (or cold and wet) on every single day, just that it tends to be that way more often than it isn't.

Climate doesn't change much. If the climate in which you live is warm and dry now, then it's probably been warm and dry for many hundreds of years—and should remain so for many hundreds of years into the future. Unless something unusual happens.

And yet climate can change over long periods of time. Scientists who study the distant past of the planet Earth know that it has gone through different periods when climates were unusually warm and when they were unusually cold. Only about 10,000 years ago, much of this planet was in the grip of an *ice age*, when sheets of ice called *glaciers* covered what is now the northern United States and central Europe.

What causes climates to change? Lots of things. One of the most important causes of climate change are certain invisible gases present in the Earth's atmosphere.

Living organisms, from human beings to plants to microscopic bacteria, need heat to stay alive. Most of the heat on Earth comes from the sun. This heat travels from the sun to the Earth in the form of visible light, the same thing that is produced by table lamps and flashlights.

On its way to the surface of the Earth, this light passes through the Earth's atmosphere, a thick layer of gases completely surrounding the planet. The gases in the atmosphere are invisible, which means that visible light passes right through them without affecting them in any way, without even warming them up.

When the light strikes the ground, however, the ground becomes warm. And when it becomes warm, the ground begins to glow. You can't see it glow because it glows with a type of light called *infrared light*, which our eyes cannot detect. Much of this infrared light passes back through the Earth's atmosphere and out into space.

However, not *all* of the infrared light passes back into space. Some of this light is absorbed by certain gases in the atmosphere—and these gases become warm. They then warm the air around them. If it were not for these gases absorbing the infrared light after it leaves the ground, the Earth's atmosphere would be freezing cold. Because these gases trap the sun's heat in the same way that the glass walls of a greenhouse do, they are called *greenhouse gases*. And the way that they trap the sun's heat is referred to as the *greenhouse effect*. If it were not for the greenhouse effect, the atmosphere would be

too cold for any living organisms to survive unprotected on the
Earth's surface.

But it's possible to get too much of a good thing. At the moment, we have just the right amount of greenhouse gases in our atmosphere for the way we live. If the amount of greenhouse gases in the atmosphere were to be reduced, the air would become colder and a new ice age would begin. If the amount of greenhouse gases in the atmosphere were to be increased, the air would grow hotter and climates around the world would become warmer.

Both of these events could have disastrous effects on the way people live. Consider, for instance, what would happen if atmospheric temperatures were to go up, on average, a few degrees. The polar ice caps would melt. The oceans would rise. Coastal cities and beaches would disappear under the waves. Some low-lying countries, such as Bangladesh, would vanish altogether.

Plant life would suffer more than human beings would. When climates change, most people can simply pull up stakes and move to areas where the weather is more comfortable. But plants are stuck pretty much where they are. Crops would die. Whole forests would wither. And the animals that live in the forests would die when their habitat vanished.

The coral reefs, which are so sensitive to changes in water temperature, would be one of the first ecosystems to go if temperatures got warmer.

When temperatures increase worldwide, we say that *global warming* has occurred. While relatively mild global warming may not bring about the end of the world as we know it, it would certainly be disastrous enough. So is there any reason to believe that such a thing could happen?

Unfortunately, there is. Many scientists believe that there will be global warming in the near future, caused by an increase in the greenhouse gases in our atmosphere. Some believe that it has

Use of fossil fuels adds to the greenhouse effect by polluting the air, as seen in this photo of an oil refinery in Texas.

The red areas on these world maps show a pattern of global warming based on a steady rise in summer temperatures between 1965 and 1990. The maps on the far right predict increased temperatures in the next century.

SUMMER TEMPERATURES

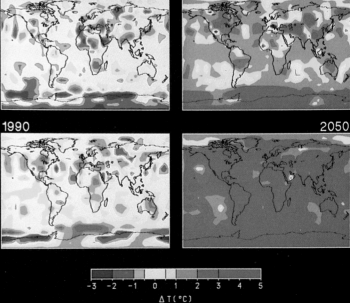

1965

2020

1990

2050

-3 -2 -1 0 1 2 3 4 5

Δ T (°C)

already begun. And the dying of the reefs may be one of the first signs that they are right.

One of the most common greenhouse gases is carbon dioxide. Although it represents no more than $3/100$ of 1 percent of the Earth's atmosphere, it is responsible for much of its warming.

Plants need carbon dioxide to stay alive. They "breathe" it in much the same way that human beings and animals breathe oxygen. When a plant breathes carbon dioxide, some parts of the carbon dioxide gas become part of the plant, effectively taking the carbon dioxide out of the atmosphere. When the plant dies (especially if the plant is burned after it dies), much of this carbon dioxide is released back into the atmosphere.

Billions of years ago, when the Earth was young, there was a lot more carbon dioxide in the atmosphere than there is today. What happened to this carbon dioxide? Much of it is trapped inside the Earth itself. Some of it has been absorbed by the ocean. And a fair percentage of it is in the remains of ancient plants.

When we dig up coal or pump oil out of the ground, we are digging up the remains of plants (and, occasionally, animals) that lived on Earth millions of years ago. These substances, along with natural gas, are called *fossil fuels*. When we burn this coal or petroleum (as we do when we generate electricity or drive cars), the carbon dioxide taken up long ago by those ancient plants is released back into the air.

People burn a *lot* of fossil fuels. As a result, the amount of carbon dioxide in the atmosphere is steadily increasing. In theory, this means that the atmosphere should also be growing warmer, because carbon dioxide is a greenhouse gas that traps the sun's heat.

Is there any evidence that this is happening? Are temperatures around the world actually going up?

That's a hard question to answer. Accurate records of temperatures have only been kept for a little more than a century, and records have only been kept *worldwide* for about 50 years. Information about ocean warming is hard to come by. But scientists suspect that ocean temperatures have been rising over the past ten years. There just isn't enough data to truly show long-term temperature trends. However, short-term trends don't look too good.

Average global temperatures have been steadily rising for most of this century, except for a period in the 1940s and 1950s when temperatures went down and another, very brief period in the mid-1980s when temperatures dipped slightly. (This latter dip is believed to have been caused by a volcanic explosion that filled the atmosphere with dust and prevented a small portion of sunlight from reaching the Earth's surface, where it could heat the greenhouse gases.)

In fact, seven of the ten years in the 1980s set records as the hottest in the century, records that are now being broken in the early 1990s. (The 1991 volcanic eruption of Mount Pinatubo in the Philippines may cause yet another brief cooling period in the early 1990s, but the rest of the decade may be even hotter than the 1980s.) In short, there's no question that things are unusually warm.

But is this warming really caused by the greenhouse effect? Or is it just a statistical accident, a period of warming that would have happened even without increased amounts of carbon dioxide and other greenhouse gases in the atmosphere? Such a statistical accident has been predicted for some time by climatologists, scientists who study the climate. This has happened before. For instance, there was a period of several hundred years ending in the early 1700s during which temperatures were unusually cold. This period is known today as the *Little Ice Age*. It had little or nothing to do with greenhouse gases.

Many climatologists believe that this current warm spell has nothing to do with greenhouse gases. Others disagree. And it's too early to tell who is right.

How long will it take to find out? Probably a decade or two, while scientists sort out the clues. Unfortunately, by that time it may be too late to do anything about greenhouse warming. In fact, it may already be too late to prevent at least *some* disastrous global warming. Scientists who believe that the greenhouse effect is already causing global warming have calculated that the average global temperature may rise as much as five to ten degrees Fahrenheit within the next four or five decades.

Five to ten degrees may not sound like much. But that's approximately the same as the difference between temperatures now and temperatures during the last ice age. That was enough to make glaciers in what is now Wisconsin. And an additional five to ten degrees could mean the city of Miami being several feet underwater.

Could the dying of the reefs be the first sign of greenhouse warming? Do we even have the time to be asking that question? Or should we be looking for a solution to the problem right now?

Let's assume that we decide to start doing something about greenhouse warming right now. What can we do?

The first step, obviously, is to stop doing those things that are increasing the amount of greenhouse gases in the atmosphere. For instance, we can stop burning fossil fuels. But that's easier said than done. Fossil fuels provide us with energy—the energy that makes our cars go, our lights burn, and our factories work. If we stopped using fossil fuels today, we would be thrown back into the technological dark ages.

But we can certainly cut down on our use of fossil fuels. In fact, everybody can do their bit to save energy. Remember to turn out the lights when you leave a room or go out for the evening. Ride a bike, walk, or use the bus to get to school or work. Every little energy savings helps to reduce the burning of fossil fuels.

But these small energy savings won't do the whole job. To further reduce the burning of fossil fuels, we will need to use energy more efficiently. We can purchase fuel-efficient cars, for instance, and keep the automobiles we already own in good condition so that they don't burn excess gas and oil. We can also buy other fuel-efficient appliances, such as special energy-saving refrigerators and light bulbs.

There are also other ways to produce energy besides burning fossil fuels. About one fourth of the electric power in the United States is generated by methods that do not release carbon dioxide into the atmosphere. The two main methods are *hydropower* and *nuclear power*. Hydropower uses the energy of rushing water to generate electricity, and nuclear power uses the heat produced by certain radioactive elements. Both of these methods have drawbacks. Hydropower can be used only in certain areas and damages the environment. Nuclear power produces radioactive wastes. Perhaps the most promising alternative to burning fossil fuels is *solar power*, which uses the energy of the sun to generate power.

Even if we cut down on burning fossil fuels today, however, the increased amounts of greenhouse gases will still be in the atmosphere. And global warming may continue for another 30 or 40 years before it stops. Is there any way to *remove* those greenhouse gases that we've already put in the atmosphere?

There might be. If the burning of ancient plants causes the greenhouse effect, growing new plants can reverse it. Through *reforestation*, the growing of new trees to replace old ones already cut down, we can build new forests. These forests will absorb much of the carbon dioxide now in the air. However, we would need to plant new trees over an area as large as the United States for this to work.

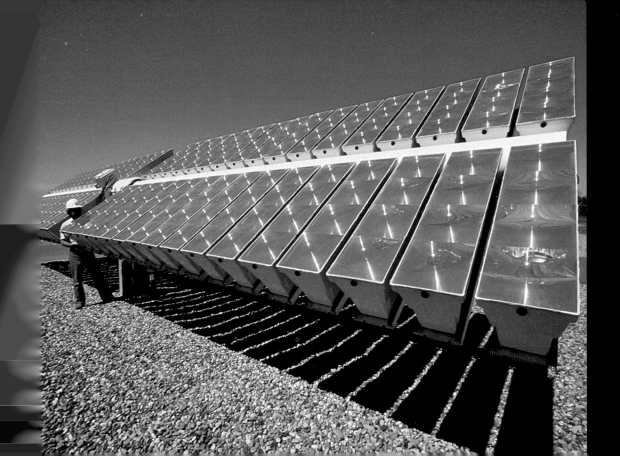

If the greenhouse effect is indeed under way—and scientists are divided on this—it may be too late to save the coral reefs of the world. One by one, they may die as the result of extended episodes of bleaching. But it is still not too late to save other ecosystems from a similar fate.

In the past, coal miners took a caged canary with them into the mine. The canary, unusually sensitive to changes in the air, would die if the air quality in the mine was bad, giving the miners advance warning to get out before they met the same fate.

The reefs may be the modern equivalent of the canary in the coal mine. But the whole world is now the "coal mine" and there is no place we can run to if conditions get worse. So our only choice is to heed the message of the dying reefs and do our best to reverse the damage that we are doing to our planet.

If we don't, then more than just the coral reefs of the world may be doomed.

GLOSSARY

Atolls—Reefs, often in a circular arrangement, found in the middle of the ocean.

Back reef—The portion of a fringing reef closest to the shore.

Barrier reefs—Reefs found more than half a mile from the shore of an island or continent.

Carbohydrates—Substances made by plants through photosynthesis.

Carbon dioxide—The most common of the greenhouse gases, found naturally in the Earth's atmosphere in very small quantities.

Carnivores—Organisms that eat animal flesh.

Central lagoon—Body of water surrounded by an atoll.

Coral—An animal that lives its entire adult life rooted to the bottom of the ocean or to other coral, its body covered with a solid skeleton; the coral animal, called a polyp, is responsible for creating coral reefs. (The term coral is also sometimes used to describe the substance of the skeleton surrounding the polyp.)

Climate—Long-term regional weather patterns.

Ecological niche—The manner in which an organism adapts to its environment, including the habitat in which it lives and the way in which it obtains food.

Ecology—The study of the interrelationships between living creatures within an environment.

Ecosystem—The complex set of interrelationships between species in an environment.

Evolved—When organisms improve over time through reproduction.

Food chain—The process by which the energy of the sun finds its way through an ecosystem; also called the food web.

Fossil fuels—Fuels, including petroleum, coal, and natural gas, formed from the remains of fossil plants and other organisms.

Fringing reefs—Reefs found between 150 and 1,500 feet (about 45 to 450 meters) from the shore of an island or continent.

Glaciers—Sheets of ice covering part of the Earth during an ice age.

Global warming—Any process by which average global temperatures are increased for long periods of time.

Greenhouse effect—The process by which heat enters the Earth's atmosphere and is unable to exit again.

Greenhouse gases—Gases that trap heat in the Earth's atmosphere, producing a greenhouse effect.

Habitat—The environment in which an organism lives.

Hard coral—One of the two major types of coral, distinguished by the hardness of its outer skeleton.

Herbivores—Organisms that eat plants.

Hydropower—Method of generating electricity that harnesses the power of rapidly flowing streams.

Ice age—A long period of unusually cold weather conditions around the world.

Infrared light—A form of light that the human eye cannot detect.

Lagoon—Body of water protected from wave action by a reef.

Lower reef slope—The portion of the reef slope below the upper reef slope.

Nuclear power—Method of generating electricity that harnesses the power of certain radioactive elements.

Omnivores—Organisms that eat both plants and animal flesh.

Photosynthesis—The process by which plants manufacture carbohydrates using energy from the sun.

Plankton—Tiny microscopic plants and animals found in the ocean.

Planula—The free-swimming larval stage of the coral polyp.

Polyp—The adult form of the coral animal.

Reef—An underwater obstacle, often a colony of coral animals found between about 50 to 150 feet (15 to 45 meters) beneath the surface.

Reef crest—The highest point of a reef.

Reef flat—The long flat portion of a reef between the back reef and the reef crest.

Reef front—The edge of a reef most distant from the lagoon.

Reforestation—The planting of new forests to replace those that have been cut down or otherwise destroyed in the past.

Reproduction—The process by which a living organism makes a copy of itself.

Salinity—The level of salt in water.

Soft coral—One of the two major types of coral, distinguished by the softness and flexibility of its outer skeleton.

Solar power—Method of generating electricity that directly harnesses the power in sunlight.

Symbiosis—The process by which two or more species live together in such a way that each provides the other with something necessary to their survival.

Upper reef slope—The sloping portion of the reef below the reef front, facing away from shore, where most of the life-forms on the reef are found.

Zooxanthellae—A type of alga that lives in the stomachs of coral polyps and related species.

FOR FURTHER READING

Bender, Lionel. *Life on a Coral Reef*. New York: Gloucester Press, 1989.

Jacobson, Morris. *Wonders of Corals and Coral Reefs*. New York: Dodd, Mead, 1979.

Johnson, Rebecca. *The Greenhouse Effect: Life on a Warmer Planet*. Minneapolis: Lerner Publications, 1990.

Johnson, Sylvia. *Coral Reefs*. Minneapolis: Lerner Publications, 1984.

Koral, April. *Our Global Greenhouse*. New York: Franklin Watts, 1989.

Pringle, Lauren. *Global Warming*. New York: Arcade Publishing, 1990.

Ronai, Lili. *Corals*. New York: Crowell, 1976.

Tayntor, Elizabeth. *Dive to the Coral Reefs*. New York: Crown Publishers, 1986.

Zim, Herbert. *Corals*. New York: Morrow, 1966.

INDEX

5752

574.5
LAM
Lampton, Christopher
    Coral reefs in danger

DATE DUE			